So I Could Fly Free

Published 2007 by CWR, Waverley Abbey House, Waverley Lane, Farnham, Surrey
GU9 8EP, UK. Registered Charity No. 294387. Registered limited company No. 1990308.

See back of book for list of National Distributors.

Editing, design and production by CWR.

Illustrations: Jonathan Lee

Printed in Spain by Zure

ISBN: 978-1-85345-434-9

So I Could Fly Free

Written and illustrated by Jonathan Lee

CWR

I had two strong wings and a lovely tail

And I had the will to win

But no matter how hard I tried to fly

The cage just kept me in

I was born and bred inside this cage

And I knew only what I saw

But I was sure there must be more to life

And I yearned to see so much more

I chirped and sang upon my perch
And my song seemed full of glee
But I felt my life just slipping away
And I longed to be set free

But then one day with my head bowed low

And feeling lonely and blue

Suddenly a stranger appeared

Saying, 'Peace I give to you'.

I lifted my head and looked into his eyes

And his eyes looked into mine

I felt like asking him why he was here

But he seemed to just read my mind

Then one day my dream came true
As my friend came close to me
With his outstretched wing to an open door
He said, 'Child, fly away and be free'

But all my joy soon faded away

As I thought of my kind gentle friend

He was still locked up inside my cage

Not a word of thanks did I lend

And so I flew on back with haste

To say, 'Sorry', and see all was well

But as I looked through my own cruel bars

He was dead on the floor of my cell

I turned my face, now full of shame

And wondered how it could be

That my perfect friend could take my place

And die so I could fly free

It was a mystery that this could be

And I flew away to hide

My freedom meant nothing now to me

Without my friend by my side

So with my thoughts on nothing else
I flew on back once more

But instead of seeing the cage I knew
It was open, with an empty floor

Then out of the blue a stranger appeared

Perched beside, saying, 'Why do you weep?'

He asked me who I was looking for

As if he could read my mind

I begged him with all my heart to tell

Where my friend was, if he'd be so kind

With tears in my eyes as I pleaded with him

He gently called my name

At once I realised who it was

My life would never be the same!

He told me not to keep hold of him

For he had not gone back where he came

But told me to tell all the other birds

That he loves every one just the same

With a joy and peace I can't explain

I flew to share what I'd been told

And as I flew the thought came to me

How his love, my cage could not hold

And when I think of his love for me

I'm sure he'll fly back to me again ...

So. I Gould Fly Free

In this book we read about a bird who was set free from its cage by another bird. This bird took the first bird's place and died so it could fly free. But he came back to life and gave the freed bird the task of telling all the other birds that he loves them too...

Colour In Pages

...This is just like what Jesus has done for us. He set us free from our sin when He died on the cross. When He rose again He gave us the gift of eternal life with Him in heaven and a relationship with God...

... Jesus could do this because He was and is God's only Son. Reveal the following MEMORY VERSE by filling in the missing Letters. John Ch. 8v36
Jesus says... 'If t__ S_n ___s _o_ fr___,
t_e_ y__ _il_ __ _e____ f____'.

National Distributors

UK: (and countries not listed below)
CWR, Waverley Abbey House, Waverley Lane, Farnham, Surrey GU9 8EP.
Tel: (01252) 784700 Outside UK (+44) 1252 784700

AUSTRALIA: CMC Australasia, PO Box 519, Belmont, Victoria 3216.
Tel: (03) 5241 3288 Fax: (03) 5241 3290

CANADA: Cook Communications Ministries, PO Box 98, 55 Woodslee Avenue, Paris, Ontario N3L 3E5.
Tel: 1800 263 2664

GHANA: Challenge Enterprises of Ghana, PO Box 5723, Accra.
Tel: (021) 222437/223249 Fax: (021) 226227

HONG KONG: Cross Communications Ltd, 1/F, 562A Nathan Road, Kowloon.
Tel: 2780 1188 Fax: 2770 6229

INDIA: Crystal Communications, 10-3-18/4/1, East Marredpalli, Secunderabad – 500026, Andhra Pradesh.
Tel/Fax: (040) 27737145

KENYA: Keswick Books and Gifts Ltd, PO Box 10242, Nairobi.
Tel: (02) 331692/226047 Fax: (02) 728557

MALAYSIA: Salvation Book Centre (M) Sdn Bhd, 23 Jalan SS 2/64, 47300 Petaling Jaya, Selangor.
Tel: (03) 78766411/78766797 Fax: (03) 78757066/78756360

NEW ZEALAND: CMC Australasia, PO Box 303298, North Harbour, Auckland 0751.
Tel: 0800 449 408 Fax: 0800 449 049

NIGERIA: FBFM, Helen Baugh House, 96 St Finbarr's College Road, Akoka, Lagos.
Tel: (01) 7747429/4700218/825775/827264

PHILIPPINES: OMF Literature Inc, 776 Boni Avenue, Mandaluyong City.
Tel: (02) 531 2183 Fax: (02) 531 1960

SOUTH AFRICA: Struik Christian Books, 80 MacKenzie Street, PO Box 1144, Cape Town 8000.
Tel: (021) 462 4360 Fax: (021) 461 3612

SRI LANKA: Christombu Publications (Pvt) Ltd, Bartlett House, 65 Braybrooke Place, Colombo 2.
Tel: (9411) 2421073/2447665

TANZANIA: CLC Christian Book Centre, PO Box 1384, Mkwepu Street, Dar es Salaam.
Tel/Fax: (022) 2119439

USA: Cook Communications Ministries, PO Box 98, 55 Woodslee Avenue, Paris, Ontario N3L 3E5, Canada.
Tel: 1800 263 2664

ZIMBABWE: Word of Life Books (Pvt) Ltd, Christian Media Centre, 8 Aberdeen Road, Avondale,
PO Box A480 Avondale, Harare.
Tel: (04) 333355 or 091301188

For email addresses, visit the CWR website: www.cwr.org.uk
CWR is a registered charity – Number 294387
CWR is a limited company registered in England – Registration Number 1990308

Prayer → "Dear Lord Jesus, thank you for setting me free. Please come into my life and make me Yours. Amen".

Jesus has set me free

Also by Jonathan Lee

Remember The Wise and Foolish Builders
ISBN: 978-1-85345-303-8

Remember The Lost Sheep
ISBN: 978-1-85345-302-1

Remember The Good Samaritan
ISBN: 978-1-85345-301-4

Remember The First Easter
ISBN: 978-1-85345-330-4

Remember When Jesus Fed 5000 People
ISBN: 978-1-85345-361-8

Remember When Jesus Healed The Sick
ISBN: 978-1-85345-363-2

Remember When Jesus Walked on The Sea
ISBN: 978-1-85345-362-5

Remember The First Christmas
ISBN: 978-1-85345-317-5

All books £3.99 each (plus p&p)

Prices correct at time of printing